Quick & Delicious Baking Recipes for All Ages

Written

By

Jake Williams

CONTENTS

INTRODUCTION

Welcome to **Quick & Delicious Baking for All Ages**, a cookbook designed to bring the joy of baking into your home with recipes that are both quick and delightful. Whether you're an experienced baker or just starting out, this book offers a variety of recipes that cater to busy lifestyles, ensuring you can enjoy homemade baked goods without spending hours in the kitchen. Perfect for families, this collection includes recipes that both young and adult bakers will find fun and rewarding.

The Art of Quick Baking

Baking is often seen as a time-consuming endeavor, requiring precise measurements, patience, and sometimes a bit of luck. However, the magic of baking doesn't always have to mean hours of preparation and waiting. Quick baking is all about finding those recipes that deliver maximum flavor and satisfaction in minimal time. From simple ingredients and straightforward techniques to efficient tips and shortcuts, quick baking ensures you can enjoy fresh, homemade treats even on the busiest of days.

Benefits of Baking at Home

Baking at home has numerous benefits that go beyond just creating delicious food. It's a rewarding and therapeutic activity that can bring a sense of accomplishment and joy. Here are a few reasons why home baking is a fantastic choice:

Healthier Options: When you bake at home, you control the ingredients, allowing you to make healthier choices. You can reduce sugar, use whole grains, or incorporate fresh fruits and vegetables.

Cost-Effective: Homemade baked goods are often cheaper than store-bought options. By purchasing ingredients in bulk and avoiding the premium prices of pre-made items, you save money in the long run.

Quality Time: Baking can be a wonderful way to spend

quality time with family and friends. It's an excellent activity for children, helping them learn about measurements, patience, and creativity.

Customization: Home baking allows you to tailor recipes to your specific tastes and dietary needs, whether you're avoiding certain allergens or simply prefer certain flavors.

Baking for All Ages

One of the most heartwarming aspects of baking is that it truly is an activity for all ages. This cookbook is designed with recipes that are not only quick but also suitable for both young bakers and adults. Here's why baking is a great activity for different age groups:

For Kids: Baking can be a fun and educational experience for children. It helps them develop fine motor skills, understand basic math concepts through measuring ingredients, and learn about following instructions. The recipes in this book include simple steps and safe techniques that kids can enjoy with minimal supervision.

For Adults: For adults, baking can be a form of stress relief and a creative outlet. After a long day, there's something incredibly satisfying about mixing ingredients, watching them transform in the oven, and savoring the final product. The recipes here are designed to be efficient, allowing you to enjoy the process without it feeling like a chore.

Together Time: Baking together can strengthen family bonds. Whether it's parents and children, grandparents and grandchildren, or friends baking together, the shared experience creates lasting memories.

What You'll Find in This Cookbook

This cookbook is divided into chapters that focus on different types of quick and easy baking recipes. Each chapter is designed to offer a variety of options that can be made in a short amount of time, ensuring you can find something for any occasion.

Chapter 1: Quick Breads and Muffins: Start your day with delicious and wholesome breads and muffins that can be whipped up in no time. From classic banana bread to savory cheese and herb scones, these recipes are perfect for breakfast or snacks.

Chapter 2: Easy Cookies and Bars: Enjoy sweet treats without the wait. This chapter includes recipes for timeless favorites like chocolate chip cookies and innovative delights like lemon bars.

Chapter 3: Simple Cakes and Cupcakes: Whether it's a quick dessert for a family dinner or a fun project for a birthday party, these cake and cupcake recipes are designed to be easy and impressive.

Chapter 4: Quick Savory Bakes: Sometimes you need a savory option, and this chapter has you covered with recipes like mini quiches and homemade pizza rolls.

Chapter 5: Baking with Kids: Specially designed recipes that are safe, fun, and educational for young bakers. From decorated sugar cookies to no-bake peanut butter bars, these activities will keep kids engaged and proud of their creations.

Chapter 6: Tips and Tricks for Quick Baking: Learn time-saving tips, ingredient substitutions, and ways to streamline your baking process to make it even more efficient.

Embracing the Baking Lifestyle

Baking is more than just making food; it's about embracing a lifestyle of creativity, relaxation, and enjoyment. With quick and easy recipes, you can integrate baking into your daily routine without feeling overwhelmed. Here are a few ways to make baking a regular part of your life:

Plan Ahead: Keep a well-stocked pantry with basic baking ingredients so you're always ready to whip up a batch of muffins or cookies.

Make It a Ritual: Dedicate a specific time each week to baking. Whether it's a Sunday afternoon or a weeknight after dinner, having a regular baking schedule can be a comforting routine.

Get Creative: Don't be afraid to experiment with flavors and ingredients. Baking is a science, but it's also an art. Use this book as a starting point and let your imagination guide you.

Share the Love: Baking is a wonderful way to show you

care. Share your baked goods with family, friends, and neighbors. It's a simple yet heartfelt gesture that can brighten someone's day.

Quick & Delicious Baking for All Ages is your guide to enjoying the many benefits of home baking without the time commitment. Whether you're making a quick breakfast, a sweet treat, or a fun project with your kids, these recipes are designed to be straightforward, enjoyable, and delicious. So preheat your oven, gather your ingredients, and get ready to discover the joy of quick and delicious baking. Happy baking!

CHAPTER 1: QUICK BREADS & MUFFINS

RECIPE FOR BAKING BANANA BREAD

Banana bread is a beloved staple in many households, known for its moist texture, delightful flavor, and the wonderful aroma it brings to the kitchen. This quick bread is perfect for busy mornings, an afternoon snack, or even a simple dessert. Its simplicity and versatility make it an excellent choice for both novice and experienced bakers. Let's dive into this timeless recipe that's sure to become a favorite in your home.

Why Bake Banana Bread?

Banana bread is a fantastic recipe for several reasons:

- **Ease of Preparation**: With just a few ingredients and straightforward steps, you can have a delicious loaf ready in under an hour.

- **Versatility**: You can customize banana bread with various add-ins like nuts, chocolate chips, or dried fruits to suit your taste.

- **Health Benefits**: Bananas are rich in potassium, fiber, and vitamins, making banana bread a healthier option compared to other baked goods.

- **Reducing Waste**: This recipe is a perfect way to use

overripe bananas that might otherwise go to waste.

<u>Ingredients:</u>

- 3 ripe bananas, mashed
- 1/3 cup melted butter
- 1 teaspoon baking soda
- Pinch of salt
- 3/4 cup sugar
- 1 large egg, beaten
- 1 teaspoon vanilla extract

- 1 1/2 cups all-purpose flour

Instructions For Baking:

1. **Preheat Your Oven**: Start by preheating your oven to 350°F (175°C) and greasing a 4x8-inch loaf pan. This ensures your banana bread bakes evenly and doesn't stick to the pan.

2. **Mash the Bananas**: In a large mixing bowl, use a fork to mash the ripe bananas until smooth. The riper the bananas, the sweeter and more flavorful your bread will be.

3. **Mix in the Wet Ingredients**: Stir the melted butter into the mashed bananas until well combined. Then, mix in the baking soda and salt. Add

the sugar, beaten egg, and vanilla extract, stirring until everything is well incorporated.

4. **Add the Flour**: Gradually add the flour to the banana mixture, stirring just until the flour is fully incorporated. Be careful not to overmix, as this can result in a dense loaf.

5. **Pour and Bake**: Pour the batter into your prepared loaf pan. Bake for 60 minutes, or until a toothpick inserted into the center comes out clean. The top should be golden brown, and the kitchen will be filled with the irresistible smell of baking bananas.

6. **Cool and Serve**: Allow the banana bread to cool in the pan for a few minutes

before transferring it to a wire rack to cool completely. Once cooled, slice and enjoy!

Customization Ideas:

One of the joys of banana bread is its adaptability. Here are a few ideas to customize your loaf:

- **Add Nuts**: Stir in a half cup of chopped walnuts or pecans for added crunch.

- **Chocolate Chips**: Mix in a half cup of chocolate chips to make the bread even more indulgent.

- **Spices**: Add a teaspoon of cinnamon or a pinch of nutmeg for a warm, spiced flavor.

- **Dried Fruits**: Incorporate dried cranberries, raisins, or chopped dates for extra sweetness and texture.

Baking Tips for Success:

- **Use Overripe Bananas**: The key to flavorful banana bread is using bananas that are overripe, with plenty of brown spots. They're sweeter and mash more easily.

- **Don't Overmix**: Overmixing the batter can lead to dense, tough bread. Mix just until the ingredients are combined.

- **Check for Doneness**: Ovens can vary, so start checking your banana bread a few minutes before the recommended baking time. If the top is browning too quickly, you can cover it with foil to prevent burning.

Enjoying Your Banana Bread:

Banana bread is incredibly versatile and can be enjoyed in various ways:

- **Warm with Butter**: Serve a slice warm with a pat of butter for a comforting treat.

- **Toasted**: Toast slices for a crispy exterior and soft interior, perfect for breakfast.

- **With Toppings**: Add a spread of cream cheese, nut butter, or a drizzle of honey for extra flavor.

RECIPE FOR BAKING BLUEBERRY MUFFINS

Blueberry muffins are a quintessential breakfast treat, beloved for their light, fluffy texture and bursts of juicy berries. Perfect for busy mornings, afternoon snacks, or even a casual dessert, these muffins are quick to make and always a crowd-pleaser. With their golden tops and tender crumb, blueberry muffins are a delightful way to start your day or satisfy your sweet tooth.

Why Blueberry Muffins?

Blueberry muffins are a fantastic choice for several reasons:

- **Ease of Preparation**: These muffins come together in no time with simple ingredients you likely already have in your pantry.

- **Nutritional Benefits**: Blueberries are packed with antioxidants, vitamins, and fiber, making these muffins a healthier option compared to other sugary treats.

- **Versatility**: They can be enjoyed plain, with a smear of butter, or even topped with a bit of yogurt for a balanced breakfast.

- **Portability**: Perfect for on-the-go, these muffins are ideal for busy mornings or as a snack packed in lunchboxes.

Ingredients For Baking Blueberry Muffins:

- 1 1/2 cups all-purpose flour
- 3/4 cup sugar
- 1/2 teaspoon salt
- 2 teaspoons baking powder
- 1/3 cup vegetable oil
- 1 large egg
- 1/3 cup milk
- 1 teaspoon vanilla extract

- 1 cup fresh or frozen blueberries

Instructions For Baking Blueberry Muffins:

1. **Preheat Your Oven**: Start by preheating your oven to 400°F (200°C). Line a muffin tin with paper liners or grease the cups with cooking spray to prevent sticking.

2.   **Mix Dry Ingredients**: In a large bowl, combine the flour, sugar, salt, and baking powder. Whisk together to ensure they are evenly mixed.

3.   **Combine Wet Ingredients**: In a separate bowl, beat the egg and then mix in the vegetable oil, milk, and vanilla extract.

4. **Combine Wet and Dry Mixtures**: Pour the wet ingredients into the dry ingredients and stir until just combined. Be careful not to overmix; the batter should be lumpy.

5. **Fold in Blueberries**: Gently fold in the blueberries, being careful not to crush them. If you're using frozen blueberries,

there's no need to thaw them first.

6. **Fill Muffin Cups**: Divide the batter evenly among the muffin cups, filling each about two-thirds full.

7. **Bake**: Bake in the preheated oven for 20-25 minutes, or until a toothpick inserted into the center of a muffin comes out clean. The

tops should be golden brown.

8. **Cool and Enjoy**: Allow the muffins to cool in the tin for a few minutes before transferring them to a wire rack to cool completely. Serve warm or at room temperature.

<u>Customization Ideas:</u>

Blueberry muffins are wonderfully versatile. Here

are a few ways to customize them:

- **Streusel Topping**: Add a crunchy topping by mixing 1/4 cup sugar, 2 tablespoons flour, 2 tablespoons butter, and a pinch of cinnamon. Sprinkle over the muffin batter before baking.

- **Lemon Zest**: Add the zest of one lemon to the batter for a fresh, citrusy flavor that complements the blueberries.

- **Healthy Twist**: Substitute half of the all-purpose flour with whole wheat flour and use honey or maple syrup instead of sugar for a healthier version.

Baking Tips for Success:

- **Fresh or Frozen Blueberries**: Both work well, but if using frozen, don't thaw them to prevent the batter from turning purple.

- **Even Baking**: Rotate the muffin tin halfway through baking to ensure even browning.

- **Avoid Overmixing**: Overmixing the batter can result in tough muffins. Mix just until the ingredients are combined.

Enjoying Your Blueberry Muffins:

Blueberry muffins are incredibly versatile and can be enjoyed in various ways:

- **Warm with Butter**: Enjoy a muffin warm with a pat of butter for a comforting treat.

- **On-the-Go Snack**: Pack a couple of muffins for

a quick breakfast or snack during your busy day.

- **With Yogurt**: Pair a muffin with a dollop of Greek yogurt for a balanced and satisfying breakfast.

Blueberry muffins are not only quick and easy to make but also a delightful way to incorporate fresh fruit into your diet. With their irresistible flavor and

simple preparation, these
muffins are sure to become
a staple in your baking
repertoire.

RECIPE FOR BAKING SAVORY CHEESE AND HERB SCONES

When it comes to quick breads, scones often evoke images of sweet, fruity treats perfect for tea time.

However, savory scones are a delicious and versatile alternative that can elevate any meal. Packed with cheese and fresh herbs, these savory scones are perfect for breakfast, lunch, or as an accompaniment to soups and salads. Their rich, buttery texture and savory flavor make them a delightful addition to any table.

Why Savory Cheese and Herb Scones?

Savory scones offer a unique twist on the traditional scone, providing a burst of flavor and versatility:

- **Quick and Easy**: These scones come together quickly, making them an ideal choice for a speedy yet satisfying bake.

- **Versatile**: They can be enjoyed on their own, with butter, or as a side to complement a main dish.

- **Flavorful**: The combination of cheese and fresh herbs adds a depth of flavor that is both comforting and gourmet.

- **Impressive**: Despite their simplicity, savory scones look and taste impressive, making them perfect for entertaining.

Ingredients For Baking Savory Cheese and Herb Scones:

- 2 cups all-purpose flour
- 1 tablespoon baking powder
- 1/2 teaspoon salt
- 1/2 teaspoon black pepper

- 1/4 teaspoon garlic powder
- 6 tablespoons cold unsalted butter, cut into small cubes
- 1 cup shredded sharp cheddar cheese
- 2 tablespoons chopped fresh chives
- 1 tablespoon chopped fresh rosemary
- 3/4 cup buttermilk

Instructions For Baking Savory Cheese and Herb Scones:

1. **Preheat Your Oven**: Start by preheating your oven to 400°F (200°C). Line a baking sheet with parchment paper or a silicone baking mat.

2. **Mix Dry Ingredients**: In a large bowl, whisk together the flour, baking

powder, salt, black pepper, and garlic powder.

3. **Cut in the Butter**: Add the cold, cubed butter to the dry ingredients. Use a pastry cutter or your fingertips to work the butter into the flour mixture until it resembles coarse crumbs.

4. **Add Cheese and Herbs**: Stir in the shredded cheddar cheese, chives, and

rosemary until evenly distributed.

5. **Mix in Buttermilk**: Pour the buttermilk into the mixture and stir until just combined. Be careful not to overmix; the dough should be slightly sticky and shaggy.

6. **Shape the Dough**: Turn the dough out onto a lightly floured surface.

Gently knead it a few times to bring it together. Pat the dough into a circle about 1-inch thick.

7.   **Cut the Scones**: Use a knife or a bench scraper to cut the dough into 8 wedges. Transfer the wedges to the prepared baking sheet, spacing them apart.

8.   **Bake**: Bake the scones in the preheated oven for

18-20 minutes, or until they are golden brown and a toothpick inserted into the center comes out clean.

9. **Cool and Serve**: Allow the scones to cool on the baking sheet for a few minutes before transferring them to a wire rack. Serve warm or at room temperature.

Customization Ideas:

Savory scones are wonderfully adaptable. Here are a few ways to make them your own:

- **Different Cheeses**: Try using Gruyère, Parmesan, or feta for a different flavor profile.

- **Herb Variations**: Swap the chives and rosemary for thyme, parsley, or dill.

- **Add-ins**: Consider adding cooked bacon bits, sun-dried tomatoes, or caramelized onions for extra flavor.

Baking Tips for Success:

- **Cold Ingredients**: Ensure your butter and

buttermilk are very cold to achieve a flaky texture.

- **Don't Overmix**: Overworking the dough can make the scones tough. Mix just until the ingredients come together.

- **Even Baking**: Rotate the baking sheet halfway through baking to ensure the scones brown evenly.

Enjoying Your Savory Scones:

Savory cheese and herb scones are incredibly versatile and can be enjoyed in various ways:

- **Breakfast or Brunch**: Serve warm with a dollop of butter or cream cheese.

- **Lunch or Dinner**: Pair with soups, stews, or salads

for a hearty accompaniment.

- **Snack**: Enjoy a scone on its own as a savory snack anytime.

These savory cheese and herb scones are not only quick and easy to make but also packed with flavor and texture. Their rich, buttery crumb and aromatic herbs make them a delightful addition to any meal, ensuring they will quickly become a favorite in your baking repertoire.

Chapter 2: Easy Cookies and Bars

RECIPE FOR BAKING CHOCOLATE CHIP COOKIES

Chocolate chip cookies are arguably the most iconic cookie around, beloved by children and adults alike.

With their golden-brown edges, chewy centers, and rich chocolate chunks, these cookies are a perfect treat for any occasion. They are incredibly easy to make, requiring just a few basic ingredients, and the results are always satisfying. Let's explore the joy of baking chocolate chip cookies, a treat that brings smiles and comfort in every bite.

Why Bake Chocolate Chip Cookies?

Chocolate chip cookies have remained a favorite for generations due to several irresistible qualities:

- **Simplicity**: The recipe is straightforward and can be whipped up quickly, making it perfect for spontaneous baking sessions.

- **Universal Appeal**: Loved by people of all ages, these cookies are a sure hit at any gathering, from family dinners to school events.

- **Versatility**: Chocolate chip cookies can be customized with various add-ins and adjustments to suit different tastes.

- **Comforting and Nostalgic**: For many, chocolate chip cookies evoke fond memories of childhood and home-baked goodness.

Ingredients For Baking Chocolate Chip Cookies:

- 1 cup unsalted butter, softened

- 1 cup granulated sugar

- 1 cup packed brown sugar

- 2 large eggs
- 2 teaspoons vanilla extract
- 3 cups all-purpose flour
- 1 teaspoon baking soda
- 1/2 teaspoon baking powder
- 1/2 teaspoon salt
- 2 cups semi-sweet chocolate chips

Instructions For Baking Chocolate Chip Cookies:

1. **Preheat Your Oven**: Start by preheating your oven to 350°F (175°C). Line two baking sheets with parchment paper or silicone baking mats.

2. **Cream the Butter and Sugars**: In a large mixing bowl, beat the softened butter, granulated sugar, and brown sugar together until

creamy and smooth. This usually takes about 2-3 minutes with an electric mixer on medium speed.

3. **Add Eggs and Vanilla**: Beat in the eggs one at a time, ensuring each is fully incorporated before adding the next. Mix in the vanilla extract until combined.

4. **Mix Dry Ingredients**: In a separate bowl, whisk

together the flour, baking soda, baking powder, and salt. Gradually add the dry ingredients to the wet ingredients, mixing on low speed until just combined. Be careful not to overmix, as this can lead to tough cookies.

5. **Stir in Chocolate Chips**: Fold in the chocolate chips by hand, ensuring they

are evenly distributed throughout the dough.

6.   **Scoop and Bake**: Use a cookie scoop or tablespoon to drop rounded balls of dough onto the prepared baking sheets, spacing them about 2 inches apart. Bake in the preheated oven for 10-12 minutes, or until the edges are golden brown and the centers are set but still soft.

7.   **Cool and Enjoy**: Allow the cookies to cool on the baking sheets for a few minutes before transferring them to a wire rack to cool completely. Enjoy warm or at room temperature.

Customization Ideas:

Chocolate chip cookies are incredibly versatile. Here are some fun variations:

- **Different Chips:** Substitute or mix in white chocolate, dark chocolate, or milk chocolate chips.

- **Nuts:** Add chopped walnuts, pecans, or macadamia nuts for extra crunch and flavor.

- **Dried Fruits:** Incorporate dried

cranberries, cherries, or raisins for a chewy twist.

- **Spices**: A pinch of cinnamon or a splash of espresso powder can add depth to the flavor.

Baking Tips for Success:

- **Softened Butter**: Ensure your butter is at room temperature for easy creaming with the sugars.

- **Measuring Flour**: Use the spoon-and-level method to measure flour accurately, preventing overly dense cookies.

- **Even Baking**: Rotate the baking sheets halfway through the baking time to ensure even browning.

Enjoying Your Chocolate Chip Cookies:

Chocolate chip cookies are a joy to eat and can be enjoyed in various ways:

- **With Milk**: Classic and comforting, dunking cookies in a glass of cold milk is always a delight.

- **Ice Cream Sandwiches**: Pair two

cookies with a scoop of ice cream in between for a decadent treat.

- **Warm and Gooey**: Reheat cookies in the microwave for a few seconds to enjoy them warm and melty.

RECIPE FOR BAKING OATMEAL RAISIN COOKIES

Oatmeal raisin cookies are a timeless favorite, known for their chewy texture, wholesome ingredients, and warm, comforting flavor. These cookies blend the heartiness of oats with the natural sweetness of raisins, making them a delightful treat for any time of the day. Whether enjoyed with a cup of tea, packed in a lunchbox, or as a post-dinner snack, oatmeal raisin cookies offer a satisfying balance of taste and nutrition.

Why Bake Oatmeal Raisin Cookies?

Oatmeal raisin cookies stand out for several reasons:

- **Nutritious Ingredients Found In Oatmeal Cookies**: Oats and raisins provide fiber, vitamins, and minerals, making these cookies a healthier option compared to other sugary treats.

- **Textural Delight**: The combination of chewy oats and plump raisins creates a delightful texture in every bite.

- **Simple and Quick**: Easy to make with pantry staples, these cookies come together quickly for a convenient homemade treat.

- **Versatile and Customizable**: They can be easily adapted with various add-ins to suit personal tastes and dietary preferences.

<u>Ingredients For Baking Oatmeal Raisin Cookies:</u>

- 1 cup unsalted butter, softened
- 1 cup granulated sugar

- 1 cup packed brown sugar

- 2 large eggs1 teaspoon vanilla extract

- One(1) 1/2 cups all-purpose flour

- 1 teaspoon baking soda

- 1 teaspoon ground cinnamon

- 1/2 teaspoon salt

- 3 cups old-fashioned rolled oats

- One(1) 1/2 cups raisins

Instructions For Baking Oatmeal Raisin Cookies:

1. **Preheat Your Oven**: Start by preheating your oven to 350°F (175°C). Line two baking sheets with parchment paper or silicone baking mats.

2. **Cream the Butter and Sugars**: In a large mixing bowl, beat the softened butter, granulated sugar, and

brown sugar together until light and fluffy. This usually takes about 3-4 minutes with an electric mixer on medium speed.

3. **Add Eggs and Vanilla**: Beat in the eggs one at a time, ensuring each is fully incorporated before adding the next. Mix in the vanilla extract until well combined.

4. **Mix Dry Ingredients**: In a separate bowl, whisk together the flour, baking soda, cinnamon, and salt. Gradually add the dry ingredients to the wet mixture, mixing on low speed until just combined.

5. **Add Oats and Raisins**: Stir in the rolled oats and raisins by hand, ensuring they are evenly distributed throughout the dough.

6.   **Scoop and Bake**: Use a cookie scoop or tablespoon to drop rounded balls of dough onto the prepared baking sheets, spacing them about 2 inches apart. Flatten each ball slightly with the back of a spoon.

7.   **Bake**: Bake in the preheated oven for 10-12 minutes, or until the edges are golden brown and the centers are still slightly soft.

Be careful not to overbake, as the cookies will continue to set as they cool.

8. **Cool and Enjoy**: Allow the cookies to cool on the baking sheets for a few minutes before transferring them to a wire rack to cool completely. Enjoy warm or at room temperature.

Customization Ideas:

Oatmeal raisin cookies are incredibly versatile. Here are some ways to customize them:

- **Add Nuts**: Stir in a half cup of chopped walnuts or pecans for extra crunch and flavor.

- **Chocolate Chips**: Substitute some or all of the

raisins with chocolate chips for a different twist.

- **Spices**: Enhance the flavor with a pinch of nutmeg or ginger.

- **Dried Fruits**: Mix in other dried fruits like cranberries, cherries, or apricots for a variety of flavors.

<u>Baking Tips for Success:</u>

- **Softened Butter:** Ensure your butter is at room temperature for easy creaming with the sugars.

- **Measuring Flour**: Use the spoon-and-level method to measure flour accurately, preventing overly dense cookies.

- **Chilling the Dough**: For thicker, chewier cookies, chill the dough for at least 30 minutes before baking.

Enjoying Your Oatmeal Raisin Cookies:

Oatmeal raisin cookies are delightful in various ways:

- **With Milk**: Classic and comforting, a glass of cold

milk perfectly complements these cookies.

- **On-the-Go Snack**: Pack a couple of cookies for a wholesome snack during your busy day.

- **Warm and Chewy**: Reheat cookies in the microwave for a few seconds to enjoy them warm and soft.

RECIPE FOR BAKING LEMON BARS

Lemon bars are a beloved classic dessert that perfectly balances tart and sweet flavors. With a buttery shortbread crust and a tangy lemon filling, these bars offer a burst of sunshine in every bite. Their bright flavor and delightful texture make them a perfect treat for any occasion, from casual gatherings to elegant parties. Easy to make and universally adored, lemon bars are a must-have recipe in any baker's collection.

Why Lemon Bars?

Lemon bars are a standout treat for several reasons:

Bright and Refreshing Flavor: The zesty lemon filling provides a refreshing contrast to the rich, buttery crust, making these bars incredibly satisfying.

- **Simple Ingredients**: Made with pantry staples like flour, sugar, butter, and lemons, lemon bars are easy to whip up without any special ingredients.

- **Versatile and Elegant**: These bars are perfect for a variety of occasions, from picnics to sophisticated tea parties.

- **Visual Appeal**: The vibrant yellow filling dusted with powdered sugar makes lemon bars as beautiful as they are delicious.

<u>**Ingredients For Baking Lemon Bars:**</u>

For the Crust:

- 1 cup unsalted butter, softened

- 1/2 cup granulated sugar

- 2 cups all-purpose flour

- 1/4 teaspoon salt

For the Filling:

- One(1) 1/2 cups granulated sugar
- 1/4 cup all-purpose flour
- 4 large eggs
- 2/3 cup freshly squeezed lemon juice (about 3-4 lemons)
- Zest of 1 lemon
- Powdered sugar, for dusting

Instructions For Baking Lemon Bars:

1. **Preheat Your Oven**: Start by preheating your oven to 350°F (175°C). Line a 9x13-inch baking dish with parchment paper, leaving an overhang on the sides for easy removal.

2. **Prepare the Crust**: In a medium bowl, cream together the softened butter and granulated sugar until

light and fluffy. Add the flour and salt, mixing until just combined. The dough will be crumbly. Press the dough evenly into the bottom of the prepared baking dish to form an even layer. Bake in the preheated oven for 15-20 minutes, or until the edges are lightly golden. Remove from the oven and let cool slightly.

3. **Make the Filling**: While the crust is cooling, prepare the lemon filling. In a large mixing bowl, whisk together the granulated sugar and flour. Add the eggs, lemon juice, and lemon zest, whisking until smooth and well combined.

4. **Bake the Bars**: Pour the lemon filling over the slightly cooled crust, spreading it out evenly. Bake

in the preheated oven for 20-25 minutes, or until the filling is set and the edges are starting to turn golden. The center should no longer be jiggly.

5. **Cool and Serve**: Allow the lemon bars to cool completely in the baking dish. Once cooled, use the parchment paper overhang to lift the bars out of the dish and onto a cutting board.

Dust the top with powdered sugar before cutting into squares or rectangles. Serve chilled or at room temperature.

<u>Customization Ideas:</u>

Lemon bars are incredibly versatile and can be customized in various ways:

- **Citrus Variations**: Substitute some of the

lemon juice with lime or orange juice for a different citrus flavor.

- **Berry Topping**: Add a layer of fresh berries on top of the filling before baking for a fruity twist.

- **Nut Crust**: Mix finely chopped nuts like almonds or pecans into the crust for added texture and flavor.

<u>**Baking Tips for Success:**</u>

- **Fresh Lemons**: Use freshly squeezed lemon juice and zest for the best flavor. Bottled lemon juice doesn't have the same bright taste.

- **Even Baking**: Rotate the baking dish halfway through the baking time to ensure the filling sets evenly.

- **Cool Completely**: Make sure the bars are completely cool before cutting to ensure clean, sharp edges.

Enjoying Your Lemon Bars:

Lemon bars are a delightful treat that can be enjoyed in various ways:

- **With Tea or Coffee**: The tangy sweetness pairs

perfectly with a hot cup of tea or coffee.

- **As a Dessert**: Serve lemon bars with a dollop of whipped cream or a scoop of vanilla ice cream for a more indulgent dessert.

- **On-the-Go**: Pack a couple of lemon bars for a refreshing treat during a picnic or lunch break.

Chapter 3: Simple Cakes and Cupcakes

RECIPE FOR BAKING VANILLA CUPCAKES

Vanilla cupcakes are the epitome of classic, timeless baking. With their light, fluffy texture and delicate vanilla flavor, these cupcakes serve as the perfect canvas for a variety of toppings and decorations. Whether you're baking for a birthday party, a casual get-together, or just to satisfy a sweet craving, vanilla cupcakes are always a hit. Their simplicity and elegance make them a versatile treat that can be easily customized to suit any occasion.

Why Bake Vanilla Cupcakes?

Vanilla cupcakes hold a special place in the world of baking for several reasons:

- **Simple and Versatile**: The straightforward vanilla flavor pairs well with virtually any frosting or filling, making these cupcakes incredibly versatile.

- **Perfect for Any Occasion**: From birthdays to weddings, vanilla cupcakes fit seamlessly into any celebration.

- **Easy to Make**: With basic ingredients and a simple process, these cupcakes are accessible for bakers of all skill levels.

- **Customization**: You can easily personalize these

cupcakes with different flavors, colors, and decorations.

Ingredients For Baking Vanilla Cupcakes:

For the Cupcakes:

- One(1) 1/2 cups all-purpose flour

- One(1) 1/2 teaspoons baking powder

- 1/2 teaspoon salt

- 1/2 cup unsalted butter, softened

- 1 cup granulated sugar

- 2 large eggs

- 2 teaspoons vanilla extract

- 1/2 cup whole milk

For the Vanilla Buttercream Frosting:

- 1 cup unsalted butter, softened

- 3-4 cups powdered sugar

- 2 teaspoons vanilla extract

- 2-3 tablespoons heavy cream or milk

Instructions For Baking Vanilla Cupcakes:

1. **Preheat Your Oven:** Start by preheating your oven to 350°F (175°C). Line

a standard 12-cup muffin tin with cupcake liners.

2.   **Mix Dry Ingredients**: In a medium bowl, whisk together the flour, baking powder, and salt. Set aside.

3.   **Cream Butter and Sugar**: In a large mixing bowl, beat the softened butter and granulated sugar together until light and fluffy, about 2-3 minutes.

Use an electric mixer on medium speed for best results.

4.   **Add Eggs and Vanilla**: Beat in the eggs one at a time, ensuring each is fully incorporated before adding the next. Mix in the vanilla extract until combined.

5.   **Combine Wet and Dry Ingredients**: Gradually add the dry ingredients to the butter mixture, alternating

with the milk, beginning and ending with the dry ingredients. Mix until just combined, being careful not to overmix.

6.   **Fill and Bake**: Divide the batter evenly among the prepared muffin cups, filling each about two-thirds full. Bake in the preheated oven for 18-20 minutes, or until a toothpick inserted into the

center of a cupcake comes out clean.

7. **Cool**: Allow the cupcakes to cool in the tin for a few minutes before transferring them to a wire rack to cool completely.

8. **Prepare the Frosting**: While the cupcakes are cooling, prepare the vanilla buttercream frosting. In a large bowl, beat the

softened butter until creamy. Gradually add the powdered sugar, one cup at a time, beating on low speed until incorporated. Add the vanilla extract and 2 tablespoons of cream or milk. Beat on high speed for 3-4 minutes, adding more cream or milk as needed to achieve the desired consistency.

9. **Frost the Cupcakes**: Once the cupcakes are completely cool, frost them with the vanilla buttercream using a piping bag or a spatula. Decorate with sprinkles, edible glitter, or any other desired toppings.

Customization Ideas:

Vanilla cupcakes are a blank canvas for creativity. Here

are some fun ways to customize them:

- **Flavored Fillings:** Add a surprise inside by filling the cupcakes with lemon curd, raspberry jam, or chocolate ganache.

- **Colorful Frosting**: Tint the buttercream with food coloring to match the theme of your event.

- **Flavor Variations**: Add a teaspoon of almond or coconut extract to the batter for a different twist on the classic vanilla flavor.

Baking Tips for Success:

- **Room Temperature Ingredients**: Ensure that your butter, eggs, and milk are at room temperature for the best texture and consistency.

- **Don't Overmix**: Overmixing the batter can result in dense cupcakes. Mix just until the ingredients are combined.

- **Even Baking**: Rotate the muffin tin halfway through the baking time to ensure the cupcakes bake evenly.

<u>**Enjoying Your Vanilla Cupcakes:**</u>

Vanilla cupcakes are a delightful treat that can be enjoyed in various ways:

- **With Tea or Coffee**: The subtle sweetness pairs perfectly with a hot beverage.

- **As a Dessert**: Serve after dinner with a scoop of ice cream or fresh fruit.

- **Party Treats**: Decorate with themed toppings for a fun and festive dessert at any celebration.

RECIPE FOR BAKING CHOCOLATE MUG CAKE

Chocolate mug cake is a game-changer for anyone who craves a rich, decadent dessert but doesn't want to spend hours in the kitchen. This single-serving treat is quick, easy, and incredibly satisfying, making it the perfect solution for those late-night chocolate cravings or sudden dessert emergencies. With just a few basic ingredients and a microwave, you can have a warm, gooey chocolate cake ready in minutes.

Why Chocolate Mug Cake?

Chocolate mug cakes have become immensely popular

for several compelling reasons:

- **Speed and Convenience**: Ready in under five minutes, chocolate mug cakes are the ultimate quick dessert.

- **Minimal Cleanup**: With everything mixed and cooked in a single mug, there's hardly any cleanup required.

- **Perfect Portion Control**: Ideal for single servings, this dessert helps avoid the temptation of overindulging.

- **Endless Customization**: Easily adaptable to suit various tastes and dietary preferences.

Ingredients:

- 4 tablespoons all-purpose flour
- 4 tablespoons granulated sugar
- 2 tablespoons unsweetened cocoa powder

- 1/4 teaspoon baking powder
- A pinch of salt
- 3 tablespoons milk
- 2 tablespoons vegetable oil
- 1/4 teaspoon vanilla extract
- 2 tablespoons chocolate chips (optional)

Instructions For Baking Chocolate Mug Cake:

1. **Choose Your Mug**: Start with a microwave-safe mug. It should be large enough to allow the cake to

rise without overflowing, typically an 8 to 12-ounce mug.

2. **Mix Dry Ingredients**: In the mug, combine the flour, sugar, cocoa powder, baking powder, and salt. Use a fork or small whisk to blend these ingredients thoroughly, ensuring there are no lumps.

3. **Add Wet Ingredients**: Add the milk, vegetable oil, and vanilla extract to the dry ingredients. Stir until the mixture is smooth and free

of lumps. Ensure the batter reaches the bottom edges of the mug.

4. **Optional Chocolate Chips**: For an extra burst of chocolate, stir in the chocolate chips. They will melt during cooking, creating pockets of gooey chocolate within the cake.

5. **Microwave**: Place the mug in the microwave and cook on high for 1 to 2 minutes. Cooking times can vary based on the microwave's wattage. Start

checking at the 1-minute mark; the cake is done when it has risen and the top looks set but still slightly moist. Avoid overcooking, as this can lead to a dry cake.

6. **Cool Slightly and Enjoy**: Let the mug cake cool for a minute or two before diving in. It will be very hot straight out of the microwave. Enjoy it directly from the mug with a spoon.

<u>**Customization Ideas:**</u>

Chocolate mug cakes are incredibly versatile. Here are some delicious variations:

- **Peanut Butter**: Add a spoonful of peanut butter to the center of the batter before microwaving for a gooey surprise.

- **Mint Chocolate**: Stir in a few drops of peppermint extract and replace chocolate chips with mint chocolate pieces.

- **Nutella Swirl**: Drop a spoonful of Nutella into the batter and swirl it with a fork for a marbled effect.

- **Vegan Option**: Substitute milk with almond milk and use dairy-free chocolate chips to make a vegan version.

Baking Tips for Success:

- **Mix Thoroughly**: Ensure all dry ingredients are well incorporated to avoid any pockets of unmixed flour or cocoa.

- **Microwave Power**: Adjust the cooking time based on your microwave's wattage. Higher wattage microwaves may require less cooking time.

- **Watch Closely**: Keep an eye on the mug cake as it cooks. It can go from perfectly cooked to overdone very quickly.

Enjoying Your Chocolate Mug Cake:

Chocolate mug cake can be enjoyed in various delightful ways:

• **With Ice Cream**: Top with a scoop of vanilla ice cream for a delicious contrast of hot and cold.

• **Whipped Cream**: A dollop of whipped cream adds a light, airy touch.

• **Fresh Berries**: Garnish with fresh raspberries or

strawberries for a burst of fruity freshness.

- **Drizzle of Sauce**: Add a drizzle of caramel or chocolate sauce for extra decadence.

RECIPE FOR BAKING CARROT CAKE

Carrot cake is a beloved dessert that combines the natural sweetness of carrots with a medley of warm spices. Known for its moist texture and rich flavor, carrot cake is often topped with a tangy cream cheese frosting that perfectly complements its sweetness. This delightful cake is a favorite for many occasions, from birthday parties to casual family gatherings, and its nutritious ingredients make it a somewhat healthier indulgence.

Why Bake Carrot Cake?

Carrot cake stands out for several reasons:

- **Moist and Flavorful**: The grated carrots add moisture and a subtle sweetness, while spices like cinnamon and nutmeg enhance the flavor.

- **Nutritious Ingredients**: Carrots, nuts, and sometimes even pineapple provide vitamins and minerals, making this cake more nutritious than many other desserts.

- **Versatile and Customizable**: You can add various mix-ins like nuts, raisins, or coconut to suit your taste.

- **Crowd-Pleaser**: Its rich flavor and moist texture make carrot cake a favorite among both kids and adults.

Ingredients For Baking Carrot Cake:

For the Cake:

- One(1) 1/2 cups all-purpose flour

- 1 teaspoon baking powder

- 1 teaspoon baking soda

- 1 teaspoon ground cinnamon

- 1/2 teaspoon ground nutmeg
- 1/2 teaspoon salt
- 1/2 cup vegetable oil
- 1/2 cup granulated sugar
- 1/2 cup packed brown sugar
- 3 large eggs
- 2 teaspoons vanilla extract
- 2 cups finely grated carrots

- 1/2 cup crushed pineapple, drained
- 1/2 cup chopped walnuts or pecans (optional)
- 1/2 cup raisins (optional)

For the Cream Cheese Frosting:

- 8 ounces cream cheese, softened
- 1/2 cup unsalted butter, softened

- 3-4 cups powdered sugar

- 1 teaspoon vanilla extract

Instructions For Baking Carrot Cake:

1. **Preheat Your Oven**: Preheat your oven to 350°F (175°C). Grease and flour two 9-inch round cake pans or line them with parchment paper.

2. **Mix Dry Ingredients**: In a medium bowl, whisk together the flour, baking powder, baking soda, cinnamon, nutmeg, and salt. Set aside.

3. **Prepare Wet Ingredients**: In a large mixing bowl, beat the oil, granulated sugar, and brown sugar together until well combined. Add the eggs one

at a time, beating well after each addition. Stir in the vanilla extract.

4.   **Combine Ingredients**: Gradually add the dry ingredients to the wet mixture, mixing just until combined. Fold in the grated carrots, crushed pineapple, nuts, and raisins, if using.

5.   **Bake the Cakes**: Divide the batter evenly between

the prepared cake pans. Bake in the preheated oven for 25-30 minutes, or until a toothpick inserted into the center of the cakes comes out clean. Let the cakes cool in the pans for 10 minutes before transferring them to a wire rack to cool completely.

6. **Prepare the Frosting**: While the cakes are cooling, prepare the cream cheese

frosting. In a large bowl, beat the softened cream cheese and butter together until smooth and creamy. Gradually add the powdered sugar, one cup at a time, until the frosting reaches your desired consistency. Beat in the vanilla extract.

7. **Assemble the Cake**: Once the cakes are completely cool, spread a layer of cream cheese

frosting on top of one of the cakes. Place the second cake on top and frost the top and sides of the cake with the remaining frosting.

8.   **Decorate**: Decorate the cake with additional chopped nuts, shredded coconut, or carrot decorations, if desired.

Carrot cake can be tailored to your preferences in various ways:

- **Nut-Free**: Omit the nuts for a smoother texture.

- **Fruit Additions**: Add dried cranberries or chopped dates for a fruity twist.

- **Coconut**: Fold in shredded coconut for extra texture and flavor.

Baking Tips for Success:

- **Grating Carrots**: Use the fine side of a box grater for finely grated carrots that blend well into the batter.

- **Don't Overmix**: Mix just until the ingredients are

combined to keep the cake light and fluffy.

- **Room Temperature Ingredients**: Ensure all ingredients are at room temperature for a smooth batter and even baking.

Enjoying Your Carrot Cake:

Carrot cake is versatile and can be enjoyed in many ways:

- **With Tea or Coffee**: Its rich flavors pair wonderfully with a cup of tea or coffee.

- **Layer Cake**: Turn it into a show-stopping layer cake for special occasions.

Cupcakes: Divide the batter into a cupcake pan for individual servings.

Chapter 4: Quick Savory Bakes

RECIPE FOR BAKING MINI QUICHES

Mini quiches are a delightful addition to any meal, offering a perfect balance of rich flavors and convenient, bite-sized portions. These savory treats are incredibly versatile, making them suitable for breakfast, brunch, lunch, or as an elegant appetizer. With endless possibilities for fillings and flavor combinations, mini quiches can be tailored to suit any palate, making them a favorite among both home cooks and professional chefs.

Why Bake Mini Quiches?

Mini quiches stand out for several reasons:

- **Convenience**: Their small size makes them easy to serve and eat, ideal for gatherings and parties.

- **Versatility**: You can customize the fillings to suit various tastes and dietary preferences.

- **Portion Control**: Perfectly portioned, mini quiches help manage serving sizes without compromising on flavor.

- **Make-Ahead Friendly**: These can be prepared in advance and reheated, making them a great option for busy mornings or entertaining.

Ingredients For Baking Mini Quiches:

For the Crust:

- One(1) 1/4 cups all-purpose flour
- 1/2 teaspoon salt

- 1/2 cup cold unsalted butter, cubed
- 2-3 tablespoons ice water

For the Filling:

- 4 large eggs
- 1 cup half-and-half or heavy cream
- Salt and pepper, to taste
- 1/2 cup grated cheese (such as cheddar, Swiss, or Gruyère)
- 1/2 cup cooked and crumbled bacon or ham (optional)

- 1/2 cup chopped vegetables (such as spinach, mushrooms, bell peppers, or onions)

Instructions For Baking Mini Quiches:

1. **Prepare the Crust**: In a large bowl, mix the flour and salt. Cut in the cold butter using a pastry cutter or your fingertips until the mixture resembles coarse crumbs. Gradually add ice water, one tablespoon at a time, until the dough comes together. Shape the dough into a disk,

wrap in plastic wrap, and refrigerate for at least 30 minutes.

2.   **Preheat the Oven**: Preheat your oven to 375°F (190°C). Grease a mini muffin tin or line with mini tart shells.

3.   **Roll Out the Dough**: On a lightly floured surface, roll out the chilled dough to about 1/8-inch thickness. Use a round cookie cutter or a glass to cut out circles slightly larger than the muffin cups. Press the

dough circles into the prepared muffin tin, ensuring they fit snugly.

4. **Prepare the Filling**: In a medium bowl, whisk together the eggs, half-and-half or cream, salt, and pepper until well combined. Stir in the grated cheese, cooked bacon or ham, and chopped vegetables.

5. **Fill the Quiches**: Pour the egg mixture into each dough-lined muffin cup, filling them about 3/4 full. Be careful not to overfill, as

the filling will puff up during baking.

6. **Bake**: Bake in the preheated oven for 18-20 minutes, or until the quiches are set and the tops are lightly golden. Allow the mini quiches to cool in the pan for a few minutes before transferring them to a wire rack to cool slightly.

7. **Serve**: Serve the mini quiches warm or at room temperature. They can be enjoyed on their own or

paired with a fresh salad for a complete meal.

Customization Ideas:

Mini quiches are incredibly versatile and can be adapted to include a variety of fillings:

- **Vegetarian**: Omit the meat and load up on your favorite vegetables, such as zucchini, tomatoes, and broccoli.

- **Seafood**: Add cooked shrimp, crab meat, or

smoked salmon for a luxurious twist.

- **Herb-Infused**: Enhance the flavor with fresh herbs like chives, parsley, dill, or basil.

- **Spicy**: Incorporate a bit of heat with diced jalapeños, hot sauce, or a pinch of red pepper flakes.

<u>Baking Tips for Success:</u>

- **Chill the Dough**: Ensure the dough is well-chilled before rolling to prevent it from becoming too soft and difficult to handle.

- **Even Cooking**: If the mini quiches start to brown too quickly, cover them loosely with aluminum foil during the last few minutes of baking.

- **Test for Doneness**: Insert a toothpick into the center of a quiche; if it comes out clean, they are done.

Enjoying Your Mini Quiches:

Mini quiches can be enjoyed in numerous ways:

- **Breakfast or Brunch**: Serve alongside fresh fruit and pastries for a delightful morning spread.

- **Lunch**: Pair with a crisp green salad or a bowl of soup for a satisfying midday meal.

- **Appetizers**: Arrange on a platter for a party or

gathering, garnished with fresh herbs for an elegant touch.

- **On-the-Go**: Pack a few in a lunchbox for a convenient, portable snack.

RECIPE FOR BAKING CHEESE AND SPINACH PASTRIES

Cheese and spinach pastries are a delectable treat that combines the rich, savory flavors of cheese with the wholesome goodness of spinach, all encased in a buttery, flaky pastry. These pastries are perfect for breakfast, brunch, or as an appetizer at any gathering. They are not only delicious but also visually appealing, making them a crowd-pleaser for any occasion.

Why Cheese and Spinach Pastries?

Cheese and spinach pastries offer several appealing qualities:

- **Rich Flavor**: The combination of creamy cheese and vibrant spinach creates a mouthwatering flavor profile.

- **Nutritional Value**: Spinach adds a dose of vitamins and minerals, making these pastries a healthier indulgence.

- **Versatility**: They can be served as a snack, a meal, or an elegant appetizer.

- **Ease of Preparation**: Using pre-made puff pastry simplifies the process, allowing you to create a gourmet dish with minimal effort.

Ingredients For Baking Cheese and Spinach Pastries

- 1 package (17.3 ounces) frozen puff pastry, thawed

- 1 tablespoon olive oil

- 1 small onion, finely chopped

- 2 cloves garlic, minced

- 1 (10-ounce) package frozen spinach, thawed and drained

- 1 cup ricotta cheese

- 1 cup feta cheese, crumbled

- 1 egg, lightly beaten

Salt and pepper, to taste.

- 1/4 teaspoon nutmeg

- 1 egg, beaten (for egg wash)

Instructions For Baking Cheese and Spinach Pastries:

1. **Prepare the Spinach Mixture:** Heat the olive oil

in a large skillet over medium heat. Add the finely chopped onion and cook until soft and translucent, about 5 minutes. Add the minced garlic and cook for another minute. Stir in the thawed and drained spinach, cooking until any excess moisture has evaporated. Remove from heat and let it cool slightly.

2.   **Mix the Filling**: In a large bowl, combine the cooked spinach mixture, ricotta cheese, crumbled feta cheese, and one lightly beaten egg. Season with salt, pepper, and nutmeg. Mix well until all ingredients are thoroughly combined.

3.   **Preheat the Oven**: Preheat your oven to 400°F (200°C). Line a baking sheet with parchment paper.

4. **Prepare the Puff Pastry**: On a lightly floured surface, roll out the thawed puff pastry sheets. Cut each sheet into 4 equal squares. You should have 8 squares in total.

5. **Fill the Pastries**: Place a generous spoonful of the cheese and spinach mixture in the center of each pastry square. Fold the pastry over

the filling to form a triangle, pressing the edges together to seal. You can use a fork to crimp the edges for a decorative touch.

6.   **Brush with Egg Wash**: Transfer the filled pastries to the prepared baking sheet. Brush the tops with the beaten egg to give them a golden, glossy finish during baking.

7. **Bake**: Bake in the preheated oven for 20-25 minutes, or until the pastries are golden brown and puffed. Remove from the oven and let them cool slightly before serving.

Customization Ideas:

Cheese and spinach pastries can be easily adapted to suit different tastes:

- **Cheese Variations**: Swap out the feta for goat cheese or add some shredded mozzarella for a different flavor profile.

- **Additional Vegetables**: Incorporate sautéed mushrooms, bell peppers, or sun-dried tomatoes for added texture and taste.

- **Herbs and Spices**: Enhance the filling with fresh herbs like dill, parsley, or basil, or add a pinch of red pepper flakes for some heat.

Baking Tips for Success:

- **Thawing Puff Pastry**: Make sure to thaw the puff pastry in the refrigerator, not at room temperature, to prevent it from becoming too soft and sticky.

- **Draining Spinach**: Thoroughly drain the spinach to avoid a watery filling. You can use a clean kitchen towel to squeeze out excess moisture.

- **Sealing the Edges**: Ensure the edges are well-sealed to prevent the filling from leaking out during baking.

Enjoying Your Cheese and Spinach Pastries:

These pastries can be enjoyed in numerous ways:

- **Breakfast or Brunch**: Serve with fresh fruit and a cup of coffee for a satisfying start to the day.

- **Lunch or Dinner**: Pair with a side salad or a bowl of soup for a complete meal.

- **Appetizers**: Arrange on a platter with a dipping sauce for an elegant appetizer at parties or gatherings.

RECIPE FOR BAKING PIZZA ROLLS

Pizza rolls are the ultimate snack for pizza lovers, delivering all the delicious flavors of a traditional pizza in a convenient, bite-sized form. These savory rolls are perfect for parties, game days, or a fun family dinner. Packed with gooey cheese, tangy tomato sauce, and your favorite toppings, pizza rolls are not only easy to make but also customizable to suit everyone's tastes.

Why Bake Pizza Rolls?

Pizza rolls have become a favorite for several reasons:

- **Portability**: Their small size makes them easy to eat on the go or serve at gatherings.

- **Customization**: You can fill them with a variety of toppings to please any palate.

- **Fun to Make**: They are a great cooking project for kids and adults alike.

- **Crowd-Pleaser**:
Perfect for any occasion, from casual get-togethers to festive parties.

Ingredients For Baking Pizza Rolls:

For the Dough:

- Two(2) 1/4 teaspoons active dry yeast

- 1 cup warm water (110°F/45°C)

- Two(2) 1/2 cups all-purpose flour
- 1 teaspoon sugar
- 1 teaspoon salt
- 2 tablespoons olive oil

For the Filling:

- 1 cup marinara or pizza sauce
- 2 cups shredded mozzarella cheese
- 1/2 cup grated Parmesan cheese

- 1/2 cup pepperoni slices, chopped (optional)
- 1/2 cup cooked sausage, crumbled (optional)
- 1/2 cup diced bell peppers (optional)
- 1/2 cup sliced black olives (optional)

For the Topping:

- 1 egg, beaten (for egg wash)

- 1 teaspoon dried oregano
- 1 teaspoon dried basil
- 1/2 teaspoon garlic powder

Instructions For Baking Pizza Rolls:

1. **Prepare the Dough**: In a small bowl, dissolve the yeast in warm water and let it sit for about 5 minutes until it becomes frothy. In a

large mixing bowl, combine the flour, sugar, and salt. Make a well in the center and add the yeast mixture and olive oil. Mix until a dough forms, then knead on a lightly floured surface for about 5-7 minutes until smooth and elastic. Place the dough in a lightly oiled bowl, cover, and let it rise in a warm place for about 1 hour or until doubled in size.

2. **Preheat the Oven**: Preheat your oven to 375°F (190°C). Line a baking sheet with parchment paper.

3. **Roll Out the Dough**: Punch down the risen dough and roll it out on a lightly floured surface into a large rectangle, approximately 12x18 inches.

4. **Add the Filling**: Spread the marinara or pizza sauce

evenly over the rolled-out dough, leaving a small border around the edges. Sprinkle the shredded mozzarella and Parmesan cheese over the sauce. Add the pepperoni, sausage, bell peppers, and olives, or any combination of your favorite toppings.

5. **Roll and Slice**: Starting from one of the long sides, carefully roll the dough into

a tight log. Pinch the seam to seal it. Using a sharp knife, slice the log into 1-inch pieces and place them cut-side down on the prepared baking sheet.

6.   **Brush with Egg Wash**: Brush the tops of the pizza rolls with the beaten egg. Sprinkle with dried oregano, basil, and garlic powder for extra flavor.

7. **Bake**: Bake in the preheated oven for 15-20 minutes, or until the rolls are golden brown and the cheese is bubbly. Remove from the oven and let them cool slightly before serving.

Customization Ideas:

Pizza rolls can be tailored to your taste preferences with various fillings:

- **Vegetarian**: Use a variety of vegetables like spinach, mushrooms, and artichokes for a meatless version.

- **Cheesy Delight**: Add different types of cheese such as cheddar, gouda, or feta for a richer flavor.

- **Spicy**: Incorporate jalapeños or crushed red

pepper flakes for a spicy kick.

<u>Baking Tips for Success</u>:

- **Even Filling**: Distribute the toppings evenly to ensure each roll is packed with flavor.

- **Sealing the Dough**: Make sure to seal the dough well to prevent the filling from leaking out during baking.

- **Proper Slicing**: Use a sharp knife to slice the rolls cleanly, ensuring they maintain their shape.

Enjoying Your Pizza Rolls:

Pizza rolls are versatile and can be enjoyed in numerous ways:

- **Dipping Sauces**: Serve with marinara, ranch, or garlic butter for dipping.

- **Appetizers**: Arrange on a platter for an easy, shareable appetizer.

- **Lunch or Dinner**: Pair with a side salad for a complete meal.

Chapter 5: Baking with Kids

RECIPE FOR BAKING DECORATED SUGAR COOKIES

Decorated sugar cookies are a timeless treat that brings joy to both the maker and the eater. These sweet, buttery cookies are perfect for any occasion, from holidays and birthdays to casual gatherings and just-because moments. Their simple base provides the perfect canvas for artistic decoration, allowing bakers to unleash their creativity with colorful icings, sprinkles, and edible glitter.

Why Decorated Sugar Cookies?

Decorated sugar cookies are beloved for several reasons:

- **Versatility**: They can be customized to suit any theme, holiday, or personal preference.

- **Fun for All Ages**: Decorating cookies is an

enjoyable activity for both kids and adults.

- **Gift-Worthy**: Beautifully decorated cookies make thoughtful, homemade gifts.

- **Simple and Delicious**: Despite their intricate appearance, sugar cookies are easy to make and taste delightful.

Ingredients For Baking Decorated Sugar Cookies:

For the Cookies:

- Two(2) 3/4 cups all-purpose flour

- 1 teaspoon baking powder

- 1/2 teaspoon salt

- 1 cup unsalted butter, softened

- 1 1/2 cups granulated sugar

- 1 large egg

- One(1) 1/2 teaspoons vanilla extract

- 1/2 teaspoon almond extract (optional)

For the Royal Icing:

- 4 cups powdered sugar

- 3 tablespoons meringue powder

- 6 tablespoons water (more or less, depending on the desired consistency)

- Food coloring (gel works best)

- Assorted sprinkles, edible glitter, and decorations

Instructions For Baking Decorated Sugar Cookies:

1. **Prepare the Dough**: In a medium bowl, whisk together the flour, baking powder, and salt. In a large bowl, beat the softened

butter and granulated sugar together until light and fluffy. Add the egg, vanilla extract, and almond extract, if using, and mix until combined. Gradually add the dry ingredients to the wet mixture, mixing just until incorporated.

2. **Chill the Dough**: Divide the dough into two equal portions and shape each into a disk. Wrap in

plastic wrap and refrigerate for at least one hour or until firm.

3. **Preheat the Oven**: Preheat your oven to 350°F (175°C). Line baking sheets with parchment paper.

4. **Roll Out the Dough**: On a lightly floured surface, roll out one disk of dough to about 1/4-inch thickness. Use cookie cutters to cut out

shapes, then transfer the cookies to the prepared baking sheets. Repeat with the remaining dough.

5. **Bake the Cookies**: Bake the cookies in the preheated oven for 8-10 minutes, or until the edges are lightly golden. Allow the cookies to cool on the baking sheet for a few minutes before transferring

them to a wire rack to cool completely.

6. **Prepare the Royal Icing**: In a large bowl, combine the powdered sugar, meringue powder, and water. Beat on low speed until the icing forms peaks. Adjust the consistency as needed by adding more water (for a thinner consistency) or more powdered sugar (for a

thicker consistency). Divide the icing into bowls and tint with food coloring.

7.   **Decorate the Cookies**: Once the cookies are completely cool, use piping bags or squeeze bottles to decorate with the royal icing. Add sprinkles, edible glitter, and other decorations while the icing is still wet. Allow the icing to dry completely before

storing or serving the cookies.

<u>Customization Ideas:</u>

Decorated sugar cookies can be adapted to fit any occasion:

- **Holiday Themes**: Use festive cookie cutters and colors for Christmas, Halloween, Easter, or Valentine's Day.

- **Personalized Designs**: Create custom designs for birthdays, weddings, or baby showers.

- **Flavor Variations**: Add a hint of lemon, orange, or almond extract to the dough for a different flavor profile.

<u>**Baking Tips for Success:**</u>

- **Chilling the Dough**: Chilling the dough is crucial for preventing the cookies from spreading too much during baking.

- **Uniform Thickness**: Roll out the dough evenly to ensure consistent baking.

- **Icing Consistency**: Test the royal icing consistency by lifting the beater; the icing should hold its shape but still be smooth enough to pipe easily.

Enjoying Your Decorated Sugar Cookies:

Decorated sugar cookies are perfect for any celebration:

- **Gifting**: Package them in clear cellophane bags tied with a ribbon for a beautiful homemade gift.

- **Party Favors**: Use them as party favors or place settings at events.

Holiday Treats: Share them with family and friends during holidays for a sweet, festive treat.

RECIPE FOR MAKING FRUIT AND YOGURT PARFAITS

Fruit and yogurt parfaits are a delightful blend of creamy yogurt, fresh fruits, and crunchy granola, layered to perfection. These colorful and nutritious treats are perfect for any occasion, whether you're looking for a healthy breakfast, a light dessert, or a refreshing snack. Easy to prepare and visually stunning, fruit and yogurt parfaits bring together the best of taste and nutrition in one beautiful glass.

Why Fruit and Yogurt Parfaits?

Fruit and yogurt parfaits have gained popularity for several reasons:

- **Nutritional Value**: Packed with protein, vitamins, and fiber, these parfaits are a healthy choice.

- **Versatility**: You can customize them with a variety of fruits, yogurts, and toppings to suit your taste.

- **Aesthetically Pleasing**: The vibrant layers make them a feast for the eyes as well as the palate.

Ease of Preparation: They require no cooking and can be assembled in minutes.

<u>**Ingredients:**</u>

- 2 cups Greek yogurt (plain or flavored)

- 2 tablespoons honey or maple syrup (optional, for sweetness)

- 1 cup granola (store-bought or homemade)

- 2 cups fresh fruits (such as berries, kiwi, mango, banana, or peaches)

- 1/2 teaspoon vanilla extract (optional)

- Fresh mint leaves, for garnish

Instructions For Making Fruit And Yogurt Parfaits:

1. **Prepare the Yogurt**: In a medium bowl, mix the Greek yogurt with honey or maple syrup and vanilla extract, if using. Stir until well combined. Greek yogurt is preferred for its thick and creamy texture,

but you can use regular yogurt if you prefer a lighter consistency.

2. **Choose Your Fruits**: Select a variety of fresh fruits. Wash, peel, and slice them as needed. Berries can be used whole, while larger fruits like kiwi and mango should be diced into bite-sized pieces. Mixing different colors and textures will make the parfait more

visually appealing and flavorful.

3. **Layer the Ingredients**: Choose clear glass jars or cups to showcase the beautiful layers. Start by adding a spoonful of yogurt to the bottom of each glass. Follow with a layer of fresh fruits, then a layer of granola. Repeat the layers until you reach the top of the glass, ending with a dollop

of yogurt and a sprinkle of granola.

4. **Garnish and Serve**: Top each parfait with a few pieces of fruit and a sprig of fresh mint for a pop of color and flavor. Serve immediately, or refrigerate for up to an hour before serving to keep the granola crunchy.

<u>Customization Ideas:</u>

Fruit and yogurt parfaits can be endlessly customized to fit your preferences and dietary needs:

- **Dairy-Free**: Use coconut, almond, or soy yogurt as a base for a dairy-free version.

- **Protein Boost**: Add a spoonful of chia seeds,

hemp seeds, or a scoop of protein powder to the yogurt mixture.

- **Seasonal Fruits**: Use seasonal fruits for the freshest flavor and best price. In the summer, try berries and peaches; in the winter, opt for citrus fruits and pomegranate seeds.

- **Nutty Crunch**: Substitute granola with nuts

or seeds for a different texture and added nutrition.

Baking Tips for Success:

- **Freshness Matters**: Use fresh, ripe fruits for the best flavor and texture.

- **Avoid Soggy Granola**: If making parfaits in advance, keep the granola separate and add just before serving to maintain its crunchiness.

- **Layering Technique**: For a more sophisticated look, use a piping bag to layer the yogurt neatly.

Enjoying Your Fruit and Yogurt Parfaits:

Fruit and yogurt parfaits are incredibly versatile and can

be enjoyed in numerous ways:

- **Breakfast**: Start your day with a nutritious and satisfying parfait that's quick to prepare.

- **Snack**: A parfait makes for a healthy snack that will keep you energized throughout the day.

- **Dessert**: Serve as a light and refreshing dessert after a meal.

RECIPE FOR MAKING NO-BAKE PEANUT BUTTER BARS

No-bake peanut butter bars are the perfect blend of sweet, salty, and nutty flavors, creating an indulgent treat that's simple to prepare. These bars require no baking, making them an excellent choice for quick desserts, parties, or a delightful snack. With a few basic ingredients and minimal effort, you can whip up a batch of these rich, creamy bars that everyone will love.

Why No-Bake Peanut Butter Bars?

No-bake peanut butter bars have become a favorite for several reasons:

- **Simplicity**: With no need for an oven, they are quick and easy to make.

- **Flavor Combination**: The rich peanut butter and

chocolate layers are a classic, irresistible pairing.

- **Versatility**: They can be customized with various add-ins and toppings.

- **Convenience**: Perfect for last-minute desserts or snacks, especially during hot weather when you want to avoid using the oven.

Ingredients For Making No-Bake Peanut Butter Bars:

- 1 cup unsalted butter, melted

- 2 cups graham cracker crumbs

- 2 cups powdered sugar

- 1 cup creamy peanut butter

- 1 1/2 cups semisweet chocolate chips

- 1/4 cup creamy peanut butter (for the topping)

Instructions For Making No-Bake Peanut Butter Bars:

1. **Prepare the Base**: In a medium bowl, combine the melted butter, graham cracker crumbs, powdered sugar, and 1 cup of creamy peanut butter. Mix until well blended. The mixture should be thick and hold together when pressed.

2.   **Form the Base Layer**: Line a 9x13-inch baking dish with parchment paper, allowing some overhang for easy removal later. Press the peanut butter mixture evenly into the bottom of the prepared dish, creating a smooth, compact layer. Use the back of a spoon or a spatula to ensure it's evenly distributed and firm.

3.   **Melt the Chocolate**: In a microwave-safe bowl, combine the chocolate chips and 1/4 cup of creamy peanut butter. Microwave in 30-second intervals, stirring between each, until the chocolate is fully melted and smooth. Be careful not to overheat, as chocolate can burn easily.

4.   **Add the Chocolate Layer:** Pour the melted

chocolate mixture over the peanut butter base. Spread it evenly with a spatula, ensuring the entire surface is covered with a smooth, glossy layer of chocolate.

5.   **Chill and Set**: Place the dish in the refrigerator and chill for at least 2 hours, or until the bars are firm and set. For faster setting, you can place the dish in the

freezer for about 30 minutes.

6. **Cut and Serve**: Once the bars are fully set, use the parchment paper overhang to lift them out of the dish. Place on a cutting board and cut into squares or rectangles using a sharp knife. For clean cuts, wipe the knife with a warm, damp cloth between slices.

<u>**Customization Ideas:**</u>

No-bake peanut butter bars can be easily adapted to suit different tastes:

- **Crunchy Texture**: Add crushed pretzels, chopped nuts, or rice cereal to the peanut butter mixture for added crunch.

- **Different Nut Butters**: Substitute the peanut butter

with almond butter, cashew butter, or sunflower seed butter for a different flavor profile.

- **Toppings**: Sprinkle the chocolate layer with sea salt, shredded coconut, or colorful sprinkles before it sets for extra flair.

Baking Tips for Success:

- **Even Layers**: Press the peanut butter mixture

firmly to create an even base layer that holds together well.

- **Smooth Chocolate**: Ensure the chocolate layer is smooth and even for a polished look and balanced flavor.

- **Proper Chilling**: Allow sufficient time for the bars to chill and set to achieve the perfect texture.

Enjoying Your No-Bake Peanut Butter Bars:

These bars are versatile and can be enjoyed in various ways:

- **Snacks**: Keep them on hand for a quick and satisfying snack.

- **Desserts**: Serve them as a dessert at parties or family gatherings.

- **Gifts**: Package them in decorative boxes or bags for a homemade gift that will delight any recipient.

Chapter 6: Tips and Tricks for Quick Baking

TIME-SAVING BAKING TIPS

In our fast-paced world, finding time to bake can be a challenge. Whether you're preparing a quick breakfast, a dessert for a party, or just craving some homemade treats, efficiency is key.

Fortunately, there are numerous time-saving baking tips that can help you whip up delicious goodies without spending hours in the kitchen. Here are some strategies to streamline your baking process and make the most of your time.

1. Read the Recipe Thoroughly

Before you start baking, read through the entire

recipe. This helps you understand the steps, prepare for any special techniques, and ensure you have all the necessary ingredients and equipment. Knowing what's coming next can save you from scrambling mid-recipe.

2.   Mise en Place

Mise en place, a French culinary term meaning "everything in its place," is a fundamental practice in efficient baking. Measure and prepare all your ingredients before you start mixing. This way, you won't have to stop and measure in the middle of your baking process, and you'll be less likely to forget an ingredient.

3. Use Pre-made Ingredients

When time is tight, don't hesitate to use pre-made

ingredients. Store-bought pie crusts, puff pastry, and canned fillings can be lifesavers. While homemade is often best, these shortcuts can still yield delicious results with minimal effort.

4. Opt for One-Bowl Recipes

One-bowl recipes reduce cleanup time and streamline

the baking process. Many cakes, cookies, and quick breads can be mixed in a single bowl. Look for recipes specifically designed to minimize the number of dishes you'll need to wash.

5.   Invest in Quality Tools

Having the right tools can significantly speed up your baking. A stand mixer or hand mixer can make quick work of creaming butter and sugar or whipping egg whites. Silicone baking mats can eliminate the need for parchment paper, and an ice cream scoop ensures uniform cookie sizes, reducing baking time.

6.   Batch Baking

If you're baking cookies or cupcakes, consider doubling the recipe and freezing half for later. This way, you can enjoy freshly baked treats with minimal effort on another day. Cookies can be frozen in dough form or fully baked, and cupcakes can be frozen without frosting.

7. Make Use of Your Freezer

The freezer is a baker's best friend. You can prepare and freeze doughs, batters, and even finished baked goods ahead of time. For example, roll out pie dough and freeze it in the pie dish, or freeze muffin batter in lined muffin tins. Simply bake from frozen, adding a few extra minutes to the baking time.

8. **Speedy Cooling**

Cooling baked goods is essential before frosting or serving, but it can take time.

To speed up the process, place hot pans on a wire rack to allow air circulation. For cookies, you can transfer them directly to the rack. For cakes, place them in the refrigerator or freezer for a few minutes to expedite cooling.

9. **Plan Ahead**

If you know you'll be baking, plan your time accordingly.

Measure dry ingredients the night before, or set out your tools and pans. This way, when you're ready to bake, you can jump right in without delay.

10. Use Lined and Prepped Pans

Lining your pans with parchment paper or silicone mats can save time on cleanup and prevent sticking. Grease and flour your pans ahead of time, so they're ready when you need them.

11. **Multitask Wisely**

While one batch is baking, start preparing the next. If you're making multiple items, look for overlapping steps. For example, while cookies are in the oven, you can be mixing the batter for a cake.

12.   Clean as You Go

Keeping a clean workspace reduces stress and saves time at the end. As you finish using an ingredient or tool, put it away or wash it. This way, you won't be left with a mountain of dishes after you're done baking.

Conclusion

Baking doesn't have to be a time-consuming process. By incorporating these time-saving tips, you can streamline your efforts and enjoy more time savoring your delicious creations. From reading the recipe and prepping ingredients to utilizing your freezer and cleaning as you go, these strategies will help you

become a more efficient and
effective baker.

Substitutions for common ingredients

Baking can sometimes feel like a precise science, but it also offers room for creativity and adaptability. There are times when you might find yourself missing a key ingredient or needing to accommodate dietary restrictions. Knowing how to make effective substitutions can save your recipe and keep the baking process smooth. Here are some common ingredient substitutions that can help you navigate these situations with ease.

1.   <u>**Flour Substitutes**</u>

Flour is a staple in baking, but it can be substituted for various reasons, including gluten intolerance or simply running out. Here are some alternatives:

- **Almond Flour**: For gluten-free baking, use almond flour in a 1:1 ratio for all-purpose flour. Keep in mind that almond flour adds a moist texture and a nutty flavor.

- **Coconut Flour**: Another gluten-free option, but it absorbs more liquid.

Use 1/4 cup of coconut flour for every 1 cup of all-purpose flour and increase the number of eggs or liquid in the recipe.

- **Oat Flour**: You can make oat flour by grinding oats in a food processor. Use it in a 1:1 ratio, but expect a denser texture.

- **Whole Wheat Flour**: For a healthier twist, substitute all-purpose flour with whole wheat flour using a 1:1 ratio. The result will be denser and slightly nutty.

2. <u>Sugar Substitutes</u>

Sugar plays a crucial role in flavor, moisture, and texture. Here are some substitutes:

- **Honey or Maple Syrup**: Use 3/4 cup of honey or maple syrup for every 1 cup of sugar. Reduce the liquid in the recipe by 1/4 cup and lower the oven temperature by 25°F to prevent over-browning.

- **Coconut Sugar:** Substitute in a 1:1 ratio. Coconut sugar has a lower glycemic index and a subtle caramel flavor.

- **Stevia:** A natural sweetener with no calories.

Use a conversion chart to replace sugar since stevia is much sweeter than sugar.

- **Applesauce**: For moist baked goods, replace half of the sugar with unsweetened applesauce. This also reduces the fat content.

3. **<u>Butter Substitutes</u>**

Butter adds flavor and moisture but can be

substituted for dietary reasons or if you're out:

- **Coconut Oil**: Use a 1:1 ratio. Coconut oil solidifies at room temperature, so melt it if the recipe calls for melted butter.

- **Olive Oil**: For savory recipes, use 3/4 cup of olive oil for every 1 cup of butter. It works well in cakes and muffins.

- **Greek Yogurt**: Substitute half the butter with Greek yogurt for a healthier, protein-packed option.

- **Avocado**: Mashed avocado can replace butter in a 1:1 ratio, adding creaminess and healthy fats.

4. **Egg Substitutes**

Eggs provide structure, moisture, and leavening.

Here are some plant-based alternatives:

- **Flaxseed Meal**: Mix 1 tablespoon of flaxseed meal with 3 tablespoons of water to replace one egg. Let it sit for a few minutes to thicken.

- **Chia Seeds**: Similar to flaxseed, mix 1 tablespoon of chia seeds with 3 tablespoons of water for one egg.

- **Applesauce**: Use 1/4 cup of unsweetened applesauce to replace one egg, ideal for moist baked goods.

- **Banana**: Mashed banana works well in a 1:1 ratio, adding natural sweetness and moisture.

5.   **Milk Substitutes**

Milk adds moisture and richness, but there are many alternatives:

- **Almond Milk**: Use a 1:1 ratio. Almond milk is lighter and has a slightly nutty flavor.

- **Soy Milk:** Another good substitute in a 1:1

ratio, soy milk has a thicker consistency.

- **Coconut Milk**: Use in a 1:1 ratio for a rich, creamy texture. It works well in desserts and cakes.

- **Oat Milk**: This is a great dairy-free substitute that works in a 1:1 ratio, offering a neutral flavor.

Conclusion

Baking is both an art and a science, and knowing how to make substitutions can make you a more versatile and resourceful baker. Whether you're dealing with dietary restrictions, missing ingredients, or simply looking to experiment, these substitutions can help you create delicious baked goods without compromising on taste or texture.

HOW TO INVOLVE KIDS IN THE BAKING PROCESS SAFELY

Baking with kids can be a fun and educational experience that fosters creativity, patience, and teamwork. However, safety is paramount to ensure a positive and accident-free baking experience. Here are some tips to involve children in the baking process safely and effectively.

1. Choose Age-Appropriate Tasks

Assign tasks based on age and skill level. Young children can help with simple tasks like washing fruits, stirring ingredients, or pouring pre-measured items. Older kids can assist with more involved tasks such as measuring, mixing, or decorating. This ensures they are engaged without being overwhelmed.

2.   Supervise Closely

Always supervise children closely. Even if they are performing relatively safe tasks, your presence ensures they follow instructions and stay clear of potential hazards like hot ovens or sharp utensils.

3.   Teach Safety Rules

Before starting, teach children basic kitchen safety rules. Explain the importance of handling utensils carefully, staying away from hot surfaces, and washing their hands before and after handling food. Reinforce these rules throughout the baking session.

4. Use Kid-Friendly Tools

Provide age-appropriate tools that are safe for kids. Plastic measuring cups, wooden spoons, and silicone spatulas are ideal for young bakers. For older children, use child-safe knives and ensure they understand how to use them correctly.

5.   Make It Fun

Turn the baking process into a fun learning activity. Use colorful ingredients, let them choose cookie cutter shapes, or encourage them to come up with their own decorating ideas. Celebrating their contributions makes the experience enjoyable and memorable.

NOTE:

By involving kids in baking safely, you not only create delicious treats but also make lasting memories. With careful planning and supervision, baking can be a rewarding activity that teaches valuable life skills and fosters a love for cooking.

THE END